MANCHESTER

YESTER

AND TODAY

BY

Cliff Hayes

A Memories Publication

Published by
Memories,
22 Crofts Bank Road,
Urmston, Manchester
M41 0TS
Fax Line: 0161 861 7775

Cliff Hayes

I.S.B.N. 1 899181 83 0

Reprinted 2004

Printed by
Ashford Colour Press Ltd
Unit 600, Fareham Reach,
Gosport,
Hants. PO13 0FW.
Tel: 01329 229700 Fax: 01329 229777

Other books by the author:

Faces and Places of Manchester - A Century Ago
Stories & Tales of Manchester
Greetings from Around Manchester
Stretford in Old Pictures
Chorlton in Old Pictures
Salford Docks
This Was Trafford Park
Stockport Yesterday and Today
Stockport in Old Pictures

ACKNOWLEDGEMENTS

Thanks go to Jed McCann, a good friend, from up there in the rarefied air of Audenshaw, for his pictures. To Barry Armstrong of Chadderton for permission to use his fine close-up pictures of buildings in Manchester city centre. Also, thanks to Gordon Coltas (Locofotos) as the book would not be complete without his railway photographs.

Thanks also go to Mike Hill of Diverse Media for backing the project and Helen Wade for the work she has put in in getting the Manchester Evening News, Readers' Local History Book Club up and running. The club can be contacted on 0161 211 2680.

INTRODUCTION

The author Cliff, with granddaughter Hannah May . . . another Yesterday & Today

EVERYWHERE changes, buildings come and go, streets become pedestrianised and whole areas are flattened. We have tried here to record those changes. Some views remain remarkably the same! Same buildings, but different uses, you do not often see corset shops, egg shops and even butchers shops are becoming rare. Today we are used to the street furniture, as they call it, the yellows lines, parking meters, balls, and other pavement adornments, and no doubt when people, in another hundred years time, look back on these modern day pictures, they will look very quaint to them.

Time moves on, with or without us, and our efforts here are two-fold. To show the past and the present side by side, and record for future generation how the city looks now. Enjoy the comparisons and marvel at the similarities as we present to you Manchester yesterday and today.

The original book was 60 pages, but when the Manchester Evening News, in the guise of Diverse Media, and Mike Hill, gave me their help and support, I decided to add another section of 12 extra pages. This gave me a chance to put forward the fate of some of Manchester's almost forgotten buildings. It gave me a chance to mention some of the issues of today as far as preservation and history in Manchester. I have tried to pull out some of the pictures that have not been used in my books before and have dug very deep into the archives to present a very mixed face to this great city of Manchester.

Enjoy your history, enjoy a great city

MANCHESTER. . . yesterday & today

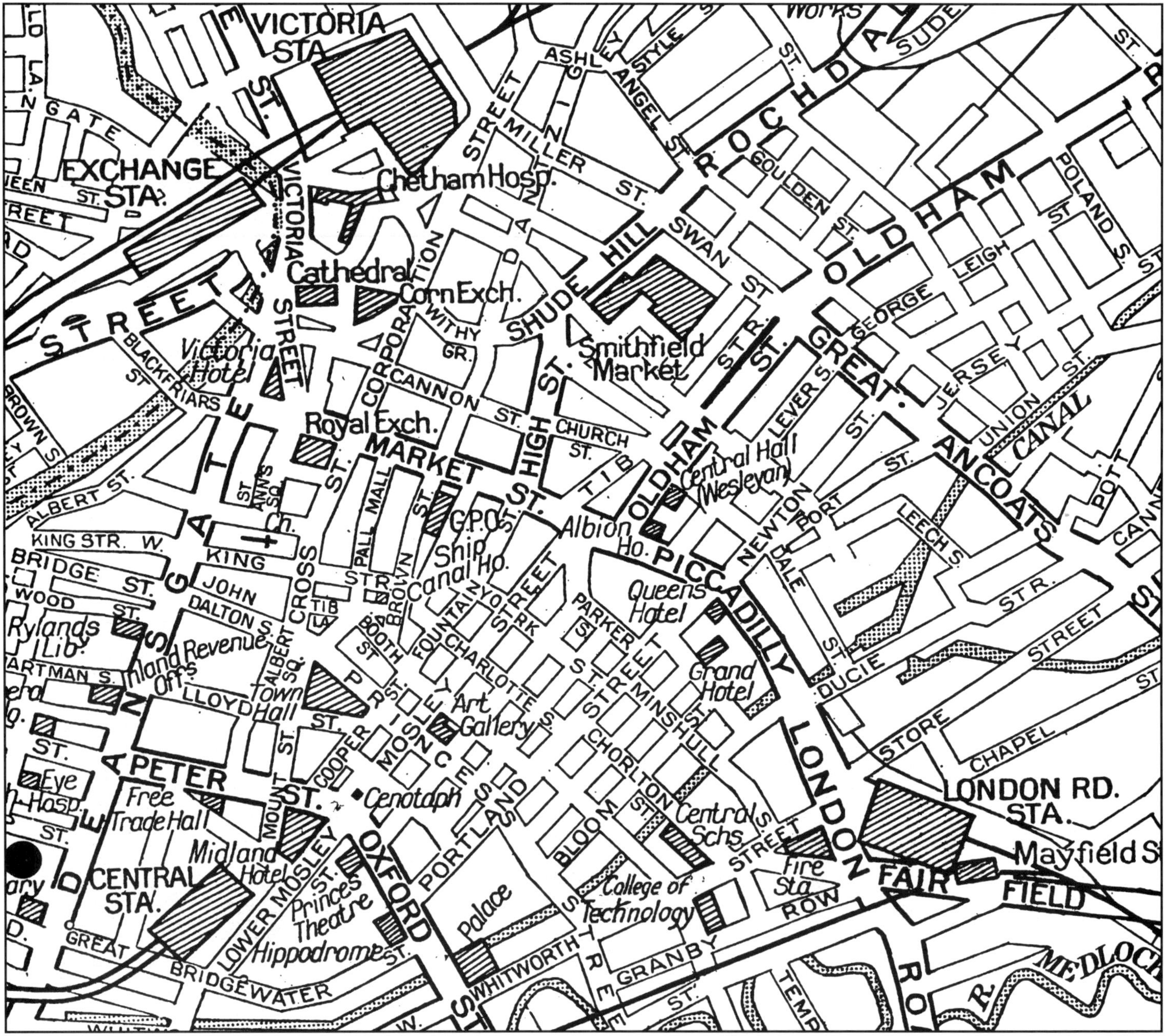

MANCHESTER CITY CENTRE 1938

Albert Square, created out of one of Manchester's slum areas in the 1860's, just to set up the monument and statue to the late Prince Regent. The prince and the square are still standing firmly in the centre of Manchester. The top photograph is from 1904 and the bottom one shows the square today.

Deansgate, Manchester, gets its name from the word 'deane' meaning 'road beside the river', and nothing to do with 'Dean' the man of the church. Above we see a view from about 1912 and below we see a still busy Deansgate, from autumn 1998.

Deansgate, Manchester, was always very popular on postcards and therefore we have a wide choice. Here we see it pictured in 1905. Above, we see two open-topped corporation trams. Right is the same view from 1996.

Deansgate, above, from a postcard from around 1906, a line of five open topped trams and a Hansom Cab waiting to take shoppers home. Below, today the Bridge St. junction on Deansgate.

Deansgate, Manchester, on a very early postcard, from over 90 years ago. Will the trams come back to Deansgate? Will the scene above be repeated? Or will it stay congested with traffic as seen below in our 1998 picture?

Deansgate, Manchester, showing the view from further away from the Cathedral. Below we see Deansgate showing the corner of Quay Street, with scaffolding around the Northern Warehouse buildings, on the right of the picture.

St. Mary's Street, and Deansgate, seen above on a view from 1933.

Right, we see that end of Deansgate in very busy mode, in September 1995.

Market Street, Manchester, and a busy scene with the shops bustling and full. Left, we see the same scene today, with Market Street pedestrianised. Rylands Building still dominates the picture.

The Midland Hotel, built by the Midland Railway Company, roughly a hundred years ago, for the very latest in convenience and comfort of their passengers, arriving at Central Station. Some may say that this is a picture of the Crown Plaza Holiday Inn, but if you ask any Mancunian where that is, they always say "oh you mean the Midland" and this is that building today.

'Poet's Corner', was really the Sun Inn, on Long Millgate, opposite the entrance to Chetham's College. It became popular with Manchester writers, who met there to read each other their latest efforts, and eventually it became known by everyone as 'Poet's Corner'. Our postcard is an early view from 1904

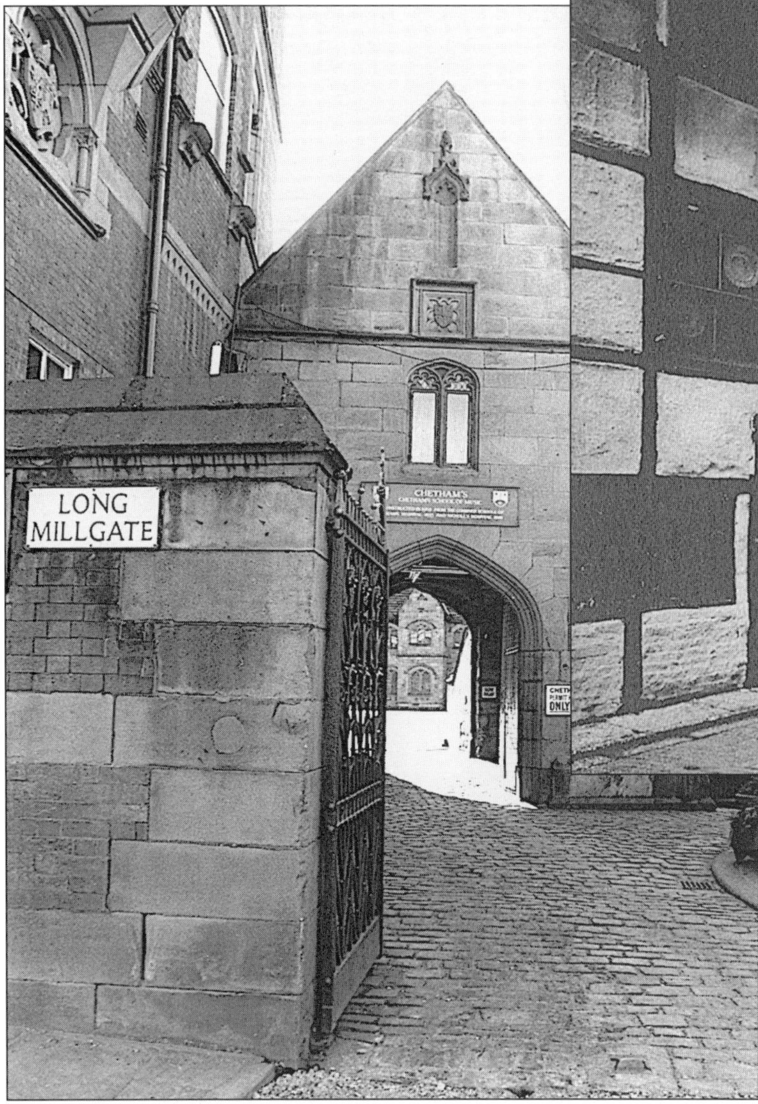

The doorway of Chetham's College as we see it today

Great Ancoats Street, Manchester, seen above in a picture from 1960. Only 40 years ago, but it seems like more. Below, on today's picture, we see that many of the buildings have now disappeared, although the Cotton Tree Inn is still there.

St. Ann's Square, shown on a card posted in 1918, although the view is definitely some years earlier. The statue of soldiers at the front of the picture commemorates those who fell during the South African campaign at the turn of the century. Below, we see the Square complete with all its street furniture from a 1997 picture.

An Edwardian view of St. Ann's Square, with Hansom Cabs at the ready. Sherratt & Hughes's Bookshop was on the right, and the Boar War Statue was still to be erected. Below we see the same Bookshop, but when this picture was taken, it had changed to Waterstones Bookshop. I wonder if our passers-by know that there are still bodies under those flags? and mind the plague pit, as you enter WH Smiths.

All Saint's on Oxford Road, shown a postcard from about 1912. Below the same scene today, though the use of shops has changed dramatically.

Exchange Station, built by the London and North Western Railway. Although it was called Manchester Exchange, it was of course, being on the far side of the River Irwell, in Salford. The picture above shows the station in about 1910 and below we see it today, used as a car park.

Oxford Street, Manchester, and above we see a view from about 1910 with a policeman directing traffic coming out of Portland Street. Left, we see the same view today.

Because of the terrorists bomb in 1996, some of Manchester's fine buildings are hidden behind scaffolding or plastic sheeting. Here are two buildings which are still waiting their transformation. Above, we see the Corn Exchange on a postcard from 1904 and below we see Thomson House, the newspaper building at the bottom of Withy Grove, Manchester, in a 1940s view, ironically with sandbags outside.

Withy Grove newspaper building, Manchester 1940.

St. Ann' s Square, Manchester as it was in about 1913. Note the the spelling mistake that Valentine's have made on the front of their card giving St. Ann an extra 'e'. The Square was created round an open space called ‘Acres Field’ c. 1700 Below we see the Square as it was in 1995.

Oxford Street, showing the Odeon Cinema, the Plaza Ballroom, St. James's Buildings, and the Refuge Assurance Building's tower in the background. Below the same scene today, minus the Plaza Ballroom.

Cross Street, and a view from opposite the Cross Street Chapel, taken in the early 1930's. This chapel was one of the victims of the Manchester Blitz of Christmas 1940, and was replaced by a smaller, more modern chapel, which itself has now been replaced with the office block we see on our 'today', picture below.

The Campfield Hall of Science, was the name given to this building when it first opened. It later became Manchester's first Lending Library, and we see it here in 1909 as Parr's Bank and Gorman's New & Secondhand Clothing Store. Below, the building is still there in good condition, but seems to be a little lost over its use. When this picture was taken in 1998, it had just enjoyed a 12 month run as the Exchange Theatre.

The Wellington Inn (the Shambles) seen on a postcard above, from about 1906. The building on the right was Manchester's Fish Market, and behind the Inn you can see the tall Victoria Hotel & Building. Below, we see the Wellington Inn in 1995, much restored and the Duke of Wellington staring proudly down from the Inn's sign.

Here we have another view of the Inn, this time from about 1950. Have you noticed that the Victoria Buildings, and the Fish Market seen on the previous page, have both fell victim to the War? Right, is a view of the Wellington just weeks before its enforced closure in 1996 after the IRA bombing. In the twelve months between our bottom picture on the previous page and this one, the Inn had been refurbished, and the Inn's sign changed.

Stevenson Square, Manchester, always second to Piccadilly as a bus station, though always busy in its own right. Above we see it busy with trams on a view from 1921, whilst below we see the buses today.

Oxford Street, Manchester, and a view from the 1920's.

Below we have a view today, showing the Whitworth Street corner and the Palace Hotel, formerly the Refuge Assurance.

The Manchester City Circular Bus, which took passengers from Piccadilly Station, to Central Station, and Victoria and Exchange, while Manchester was waiting for the Pic-Vic Underground to be built. The project was never completed, and thank goodness the trams arrived in time.

John Rylands was a good man, you could even say, a great man, and he was definitely a modest man. Even today the good that he did quietly over 100 years ago keeps popping up. Above we see the John Rylands Library given to the City of Manchester by his widow, Enriqueta, at the turn of the century. She insisted on the finest building materials throughout, and the building still looks a credit to his memory today as we see on the right. There are guided tours of the building most Wednesdays; well worth the effort.

St. Peter's Square, with the Midland Hotel dominating our view from around 1907. The church has gone yet the war that will be commemorated by a Centotaph has not begun yet. The old buildings that were swept away to make way for Central Library are there on the right. The hotel is the only thing still there on our today picture below, and it's still the Midland is most people's minds.

The Portland Street corner of Piccadilly, Manchester, and the no. 11x wait to start it's journey to Old Trafford, probably on a match special in the 1950s. Reconstruction work in Piccadilly is going on behind our bus. Today, below that work has been completed and Piccadilly traffic flows well.

A lovely view of Piccadilly Gardens, taken in 1962. The department store is still Rylands, built in 1930 and awaiting the change to Pauldens and then Debenhams. The sunken gardens look in lovely condition and the whole place has an 'open' look about it. The statues of Piccadilly tell a story in history and though we do not appreciate them, as we should, they are there, as our today picture shows clearly. That is the Duke of Wellington gazing down as people cross the wide traffic lanes. He's been there since August 30th, 1856 and his was the second statue to be erected in Manchester.

A very old photograph of Piccadilly, Manchester, taken from the Queen's Hotel which stood on the corner of London Road. That's the Infirmary and Mental Asylum on the left of our picture, and Queen Victoria's statue was still to arrive. Today the trams have cut the far side of Piccadilly off from general traffic. This road we see here was built as Lever's Row and the name Piccadilly was first used almost 200 years ago.

A view of Manchester's Town Hall as it appeared over a hundred years ago, yes 1889, more than a century ago. The town hall opened in 1877 to a design by Alfred Waterhouse and has served Manchester well over the last 120 years. All the transport is horse drawn, and the statues of Oliver Heywood and John Bright have still to join the august body in the square. Below we see the square from the same spot in March of 1998.

An unusual view of the Town Hall, being taken from Cross Street corner from about 1914. When we look at modern pictures of the town hall we can date them from what is being advertised or promoted in Albert Square. Our today picture is just a few years old, showing the town hall during our bid for the Olympic Games, that will be held in the year 2000.

Manchester Cathedral, shown from a postcard of 1904. The porch on the front looks cleaner because it has just been added to the church. The grounds of Chetham's College can be clearly seen on the left. Below we see the cathedral today and the porch has blended in during the 90 years between our pictures. There has been a place of worship here for a thousand years, a fact that does not seem to be generally known.

Right we see a 1906 view of the Cathedral of Manchester, and we see the Cromwell statue in the middle of Deansgate. It got the nickname 'the Pedestrian's Friend' because it gave a resting place for those crossing the busy road. Today it's difficult to park near to the Cathedral, but more of us should make the effort to visit the Cathedral Church of St. Mary, St. George and St. Denys, (to give the church it's full title). It is steeped in history, mystery, stories from the past, great men and women, and of course religion.

It seems a long time ago, yet this is this Corn Exchange from 1990. The strange triangular building that once stood in front of it has gone, and a fountain had replaced it. The 'Manchester Products and Corn Exchange' looks older than it really is, being only a hundred years old. The very latest in hydrolic lifts, water powered, from the Pump House on Bridge Street, were installed to lift the produce to the market floor. That market floor became a wonderful browsers' delight when it was turned into small units, and you could have your fortune told as well as swap comics, buy old medals, postcards and books. Fennel Books (John) was one of the great shops in there. On our picture to the right we see Steve, who ran the Movie Store, waiting to grab a passing customer on a quiet day in 1992.

I have tried to not dwell on the effects of the IRA bomb on this part of Manchester. It will be the subject of a whole photographic book one day - before and after the I.R.A. bomb, but the re-building cannot be ignored.

Two more pictures that could almost be 'today' pictures, and yet are now consigned to the 'yesterday' part of our memories. Above we see the very bottom of Market Street, looking from St. Mary's Gate. Officially Market Street ran to St. Ann's Square corner. Marks and Spencer's, with its distinctive canopy, which took the blast of the 1996 bomb, is on the left in this photograph from March of that year. Below we see Shambles Square in 1995, how pleasant it was to sit outside with a pint.

Above we see Oxford Street and the Palace theatre on a 1911 view. In 1913 the Palace Theatre was rebuilt and lost the towers and ornate front we see here.

Left we look at that part of Oxford Street today with its one way traffic system. For the uninitiated it is Oxford Street until the corner of Charles Street, by the BBC front door, and then it becomes Oxford Road, don't ask me why though.

'The Rover's Return Market Place' in 1897 says the caption on our photograph above. The market was at the top of Withy Grove, at the start of Shude Hill, and was, for over 200 years, a very busy one. Below we see that same view today and the market gone replaced by a ramp from the multi-storey parking.

Here is an unusual picture, taken from the top of the spiral ramp just after it had been completed in about 1985. I was terrified the first time I drove down it, it was like a helter-skelter ride in a car. You can see that work had not started on the tram lines that now pass over Shude Hill, which swept away many of the older building. Below we are still in the past, in the 1950s, and browsing for books on Morten's Bookstall that stood here for many years. The bookstall is still around, and just outside Yates's on High Street.

Another view of the little market that drew bargain hunters from all over Manchester. I worked at Thompson House for over ten years and loved to call at Tony's stall and see if I could pick up bargain in L.P.'s (vinyl to you). Here we see Tony's record stall from, I think, the early 60's with the Mosley Arms behind it, and Morton's Radio shop next to it. Did you notice the change of spelling for the name. Below we see the corner of Dantzig Street and Withy Grove from 1996.

Left we see the headquarters of the Co-Operative Insurance Society, that stood on the Corporation Street, where it joined Cheetham Hill Road. You can just make out the company's name on the front of the building

Right we see the building used in 1997 as an hotel. Parker's Hotel and the large rooms created for Board Meetings, made great function rooms.

Swan Street, showing the corner of Oldham Road, from around 1970. The church you see was St. Paul's, built in 1878, and at one time was a busy and well attended church. It had been the headquarters of the 'Samaritans' when they first appeared in Manchester, but now we see it minus it's roof and ready to be pulled down. Below the same view today, but the church has gone, but the bank is still there on the corner even if it has changed ownership.

Manchester's Royal Exchange, as it was in 1910. The columned entrance was taken down when the building was enlarged, starting in 1914. Work was interrupted by the Great War and not completed until 1921. The building got its Royal prefix after a visit by Queen Victoria in 1851. Below is a picture of that same view today, with the Arndale Centre stretching across Market Street.

Looking up King Street from Cross Street, from a very early postcard c. 1903. The old Town Hall building is still there on the right, and the Lancashire and Yorkshire Insurance building at the top of the street.

Right, we see the view today, and a Lloyd's Bank was built to replace the old Town Hall, and those columns you see on the view above are still around in Heaton Park. The top of the street looks the same, but everything on the way up the street has changed.

Above we see the entrance slope to London Road Station, Manchester, caught on a postcard from 1913. This railway station had opened on May 10th, 1842, by the London North Western Railway. The station was rebuilt and renamed Piccadilly in September 1960, the same day that electric locos started their share of the service to London (Euston).

Right, we see the bottom of that slope today, still plenty of taxis there waiting for passengers.

Above is a photograph of London Road Railway Station, taken about 90 years ago. Notice how the goods side of the business has developed, and a receiving yard and warehouse can be seen on the left of the picture.

Right we see the exact same view today, complete with today's bus going past. The warehouse has been replaced with the office buildings, including the Blood Transfusion Service and Ian Allen's Bookshop.

The scene at Manchester Central Railway Station in October 1950. The first Manchester Central station opened in 1877 but it was not the station seen here, but a temporary one at the side of Watson Street. This station opened on July 1st 1880, and just for the record, closed on May 4th, 1969. Below, we see the station as it is now, used as the Greater Manchester Exhibition and Event Centre and busy with exhibitions, concerts, etc.,

Central Station Manchester, taken about a hundred years ago. You can see the covered walkway between the station and the Midland Hotel, which stopped travellers from getting wet. Not that it rained in Manchester in those days. There was also a ramp inside the station that led to a tunnel under the road and into the Midland Hotel basement, to convey the luggage. I wonder if that's still there today behind some locked door? The photograph below, taken in 1995, has caught people reading what is the next exhibition, where once they scanned timetables for the next train.

Locofotos

A 1950's picture of a British Railways loco no. 9343 on shunting duty at Manchester Central Station. Below we see 55002, one of the wonderfully powerful Deltic diesel locomotives bringing in a Liverpool-York-Newcastle express into Manchester Victoria Station in the late 1960s. Cross country services had buffet cars and restaurant facilities in those days, not just a trolley and pretend cups of tea, as today.

Locofotos

Jubilee class engine no. 45700 "Amethyst" pulls out Manchester Victoria Station with the express to Carlisle on a Summer Saturday of May 5th, 1962.

We still get the odd steam train going through Manchester. Below we see a visit to 'The Museum of Science and Industry' by the most famous of all steam locos, 'Flying Scotsman', on April 18th, 1987. Yes, that's me infront of the engine, smiling at the camera, and the grey haired gent with his back to the camera is Dr. Hills, the museum's curator at the time, and a great man.

Here we recall those halcyon days before bus de-regulation day (known in the transport industry as the second D-Day). No one will believe the stories of that day buses going the wrong way and passengers guiding the drivers. Confused drivers stopping and asking passers-by which way the no. XX bus usually went. Oh! we did laugh as we stood at the bus stop waiting. Above is the No. 23 almost at it's destination, Piccadilly. Below we see the busy scene on Corporation Street in the 1950. Buses no. 75 and 81 head for Albert Square, while the 17x provides a rush-hour service.

The trolley bus was once an intrinsic part of Manchester's transport system, if mainly to east Manchester. It's a forgotten part of that history, but here we see two of those trolley buses in Piccadilly, Portland St., waiting to return to Denton in 1960. The last trolley bus in Manchester area ran on New Years Eve of 1966 and was by Ashton Corporation.

Electric traction will always be cheaper and cleaner than diesel or petrol engines and the return of the trams meant the first step in lightening the burden on our streets. Here, the Manchester Evening News tram threads it's way down Mosley Street in 1998.

We cannot look at the Manchester of yesterday and today and ignore the wonderful restoration of the Castlefield area. Leading from the front, and by example, it has been transformed from a dingy area of coal yards and dirt, to the in-place and a great watering-hole. Jim Ramsbottom has lead that revival, and fought tooth and nail for the re-birth of Castlefield. Above we see the scene on a busy and sunny summer day in 1990 when a Barge Festival was held. Whilst left, we see sunken barges and the dereliction that marred the area in the early 1970's

A view of the Bridgewater Canal Basin taken in 1892. Below, we see a peaceful and tranquil scene from 1997. The 'Dukes '92', made out of the original stables of the Bridgewater Canal Co. has a very good reputation for food, especially its cold buffet lunches. Called 'Dukes '92' because it is beside the 92nd lock on the Rochdale Canal, it has recently been enlarged and is recommended for a visit.

Gorton Monastery, or as it is officially, the church of St. Francis at Gorton, as it was seen on a photograph from about 1950. This church is fairly unique, as it is a church designed by E. W. Pugin, but built by local labour and with bricks made locally, as far as the friars living quarters were concerned. It lay empty and derelict for some years, and as scheme after scheme failed for the use of the building, hope sank and the place looked doomed. Now a Monastery Trust has taken over, plans are in place to not only save the building, but turn it into a high-tech centre for study. I think they will succeed, and I know they have the good wishes of all, behind their venture. Just to prove it's still there, we see the church on an open day in 1998.

POSTSCRIPT

There is a lot of debate about Manchesters buildings and the decisions are definitely not being influenced as they should by the people, who matter, the people who pay their rates, who use these buildings, and who have to look at whatever goes up in their place. We seem to be told that it would be alright to pull the whole of Manchester down and rebuild it as sky scrapers, "Think of the jobs it would create" we read. "And it won't cost the tax-payer anything", we are assured. Some developers seem to think that if they save just a few bricks on the outside of a listed building, then it gives them the right to put up a 20-storey office block adjoining it, and it's all right to turn a light and airey street into constant shadow.

I have long been an admirer of the work of photographer Barry Armstrong, and he has produced many of the 'today' photographs in this book. The collage above, he produced from many of those pictures. This, really took my breath away. I think it is fantastic, and I include it here, purely as a whim, and a pleasure to look at.

Manchester's Free Trade Hall, as it was in 1996, restored, as we can read from the plaque on the left, after being bombed during W.W.2. This frontage was built in 1857 to a design by Walters. I just cannot understand why the Council thought they needed to close the Hall. I known the Hallé have gone off to their new shiny hall, but it wasn't just used by them, it was used by hundreds of small organisations, many of whom can't afford the new charges at the Bridgewater Hall. The Manchester Evening News has twice carried appeals from organisations looking for somewhere to hold concerts or meetings. I was told the Free Trade Hall ran at a profit, so why not open it again for Public Use. Every time I go past there seems to be someone using it. Granada recently used it for rehersals, as did the Royal Exchange Theatre Company, so why don't they open a diary, and start taking bookings again? The Free Trade Hall, is after all part of the fabric of Manchester, and the people of Manchester.

This mural, by Mr A Sherwood Edwards, is inside the foyer to the main hall of the Manchester Free Trade Hall. It depicts of course, 'Peterloo' which happened, more or less on the site of the hall. There is a book that tells the story of the great men and great deeds that have echoed throughout this hall. The ghosts' of the many passionate and eminent speakers who have stood in this hall, and changed history for ever, would certainly have a lot to say about the way the hall is being treated today!

Now I'm really not one who thinks we must live in the past, but we need reminding of mistakes made in the past, and triumphs too. If we do not heed the mistakes of history, then we will just keep making the same mistakes. People fighting for justice and recognition today can take heart, from those who fought and won in the years gone by. Pardon those 'Shot At Dawn', 'Justice for C.J.D. Sufferers', compensation for those who suffer due to blood transfusions, there are many fights today that have a similar one in the past and how many are closely connected with this building. It's strange to think that some M.P. once got up on the F.T.H. stage and said "It would be dangerous to give the vote to women, they wouldn't know what to do with it!", and he was clapped. Oswald Mosley once stood here and told the audience that we should back Hitler's Germany, and selective breeding wasn't such a bad thing, Manchester stood up to him that time. The Free Trade Hall reminds us that Governments and Councils, though elected by the people, don't always know what's best for those people.

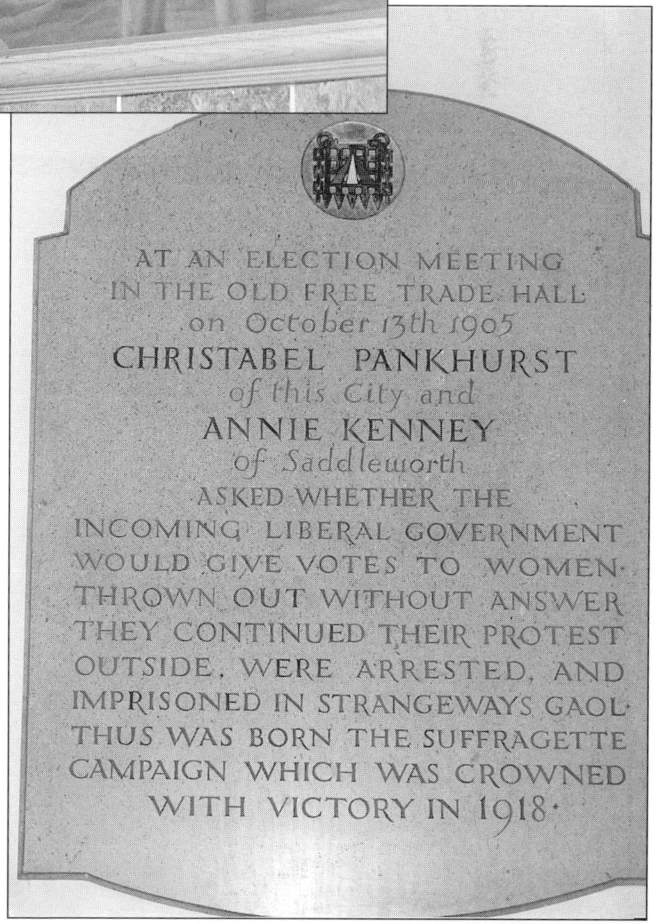

Charter Street Ragged School, shown above from a recent photograph. Some years ago it was a pleasure to show visitors round the school, and show them how it was run. Schools like this were built so that children from this and other poor areas of Manchester were given a chance, to at least learn to read and write. We would sit visiting children down on the stark benches and give them slates to write on, so they could see for themselves how schools used to be. Now we have to trail up to Wigan Pier or down to Styal Mill to be able to do this. Unfortunately, in the end, Charter Street School closed down for lack of funds, and help from the authorities, and Manchester lost another vital piece of history.

Right: The Corn Exchange as it looked from Cateaton Street, just a month before the I.R.A. bomb tore this bit of Manchester apart. Opened in 1904 the building was being put to good use, and was a facinating mixture of arty-craft shop, junk stalls, antiques, lots of little outlets that you would not find anywhere else. Above, and around the Exchange Floor was a labrinth of corridors, with hundreds of offices, where many small businesses thrived. I doubt we will see it, or its like again.

New Cross Corner, Ancoats, and the scene in 1994, just after the Crown and Kettle Inn had closed. The inside of this pub was panelled, and some of the wood used was taken from the R100, one of the great airships that flew earlier this century. Owned by Express Newspapers, it was due to be converted into extra offices, but the plan never went through, and still stands there today, awaiting it's fate.

Right: we see a building on Great Ancoats Street, next to what was the Daily Express building. How this building is still standing is both a miracle and a tribute to it's original builders. It was constructed as the 'Night Shelter for Homeless and Fallen Women' by the Methodist Movement, and served this purpose for many years. I was told that the windows were deliberately small so as to deter anyone climbing in or out of them. This listed building was latterly a union office connected with the printing unions at the Daily Express (N.A.T.S.O.P.A., I think) It is now owned by whoever owns the Express building next door.

Above we see St. John's Gardens, that lie between Byrom Street and Lower Byrom Street, off Deansgate, Manchester. The church that once stood here was founded by Edward Byrom, and it was his daughter Eleanor who made sure that the land would never be built upon. When she died in 1838 she left over £4,000 to different charities in the town. Many noteworthy people rest beneath these paths and seats, including John Owen (Owen's College) and Manchester's Ice Maiden, Lavinia Robinson.

The Reform Club, one of the successes of redevelopment in Manchester. Built as a retreat for the great 'Liberal' minds of the last century, it has been tastefully redeveloped by Bruntwood, and has a rosey future as a restaurant and offices. This building was known for many years as the Manchester Club and was the scene of many sporting social events.

St. Bede's College, Alexandra Road, Moss Side, and built as the Manchester Aquarium in 1880. It had great glass fronted tanks full of fish for public view, and was a great success when it first opened. When this venture failed, Bishop Vaughan, RC Bishop of Salford, led a movement to purchase the building, which they did, and it was turned into the College it is today. The building was never finished to its original plans, and the entrance porch that we see here should have been in the middle of a longer facade.

Right: There was once a Catholic Chapel in Camp Street, off Deansgate, which served the masses packed in the alleys and courtyards that abounded in that area. The skylights would have let much need light into the small chapel, and you can just about make out the blocked-up window and doorway at the front.

The inside of the hall, taken a few years ago, and showing the missing floor, and what once was a lovely oak beamed wall.

Baguley Hall, Hall Lane, Baguley. This must be the oldest building in Greater Manchester, and yet it is shut up and falling into disrepair. It is a medieval secular building, and of considerable national interest. A timber framed 14th century building, it was used for many years as a farmhouse, and then as a storage depot, subsequently it missed out on any redevelopment that would have happened had it been a family home. When acquired by Manchester Council, it was renovated, and quite a lot of money was spent on bringing it to a good state of preservation. It was then handed over to the Ministry of Public Buildings and Works, who seemed at a loss to know what to do with it. English Heritage own it now, and as we write it is being offered to anyone, for almost any use, as long you take over the responsibility of the structure of the building. Over the years there have been some unlucky developments here, such as the 14th century flag-stone floor in the great hall that was taken up and left outside, and then vanished over-night. And when removing panels from an upstairs room somebody painted numbers on the front of them so they could be put back in their correct place, unfortunately, the numbers were painted in gloss paint have proved almost impossible to remove. And many more acts of sheer vandalism are destroying further, this lovely old hall.

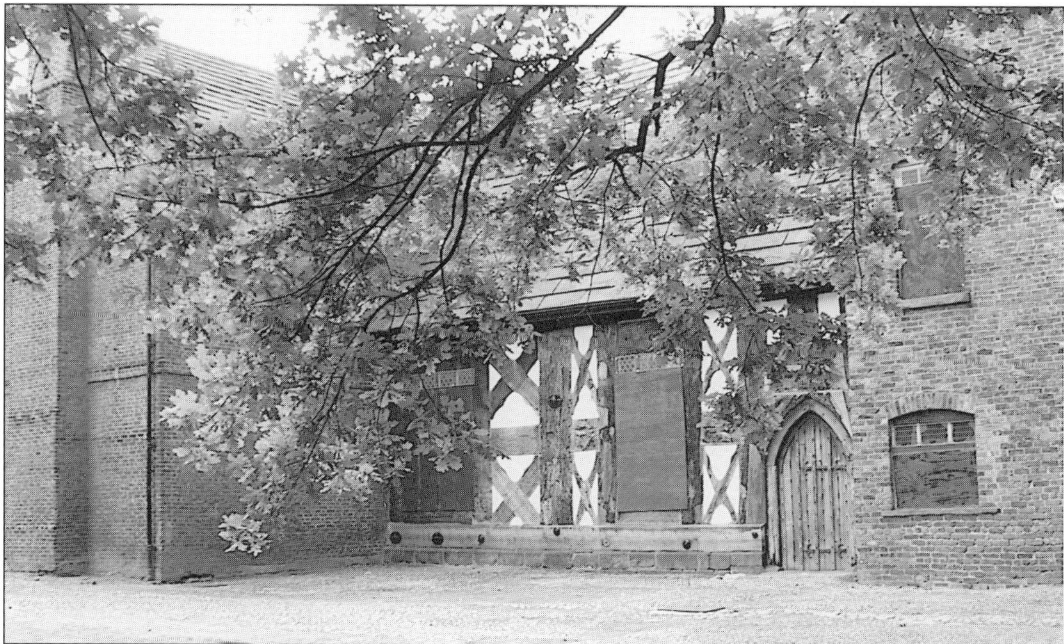

Here we see the back of Baguley Hall, and you can appreciate even more the timber framed construction that makes this hall unique. There are some architectural historians who think that this part of the hall shows signs of being even earlier than the 14th century.

Right: we see some of the flag-stones and original timbers from the hall stored at the back. Since Newall Green School closed down, vandalism at the hall has reduced dramatically, and there is now permanent security on the premises. But what of the future? Will it go like so many other old buildings, left to rot, then be pulled down through lack of money, the land sold, and new houses put up.
Will English Heritage allow that to happen?

Hough End Hall, off Mauldeth Road, Chorlton, built in about 1600 by Sir Nicholas Mosley, when he purchased the Lordship of the Manor of Manchester. Said to be built on the site of an earlier house where his father was born. This lovely Elizabethan building, has served as both a Manor House and a Farm House, nicknamed Peacock farm. Unfortunately, its fate was sealed when they built a seven storey office block only feet away from its front door. In its recent past it has been used as a night-club, pub and restaurant, and today, is once again offered for sale.

Left: Here we see the old night entrance to the hall, with the small round window, for the servants to watch out for their master's return.

'When will we see you again?' that is the question hanging over the Wellington, now taken down from its original site in the Shambles, and is at the moment being reconstructed under a plastic tent in Cathedral Street. Unfortunately the site chosen is six foot narrower than the original width of the pub, perhaps it works out differently in centimetres.

Right: A nice 1995 picture of Sinclair's Oyster Bar and how it served the shoppers at that well known store.

The Victoria Baths, on Hathersage Road, Rusholme. The battle is now on to save this magnificent and unique building. It could well be turned into an Arts & Craft Centre, who knows, but this is certainly a building well worth preserving.

Right: Here we see a picture of the inside of what is perhaps Manchester's greatest gem, Chetham's Library. Here they have safely gathered in and look after so much of Manchester's past. It is an honour to visit it, and yet so many people do not know that it is there, and that they can visit it.